New Rules For Relationships and Modern Marriage:
Love Is Not Enough!

By

Paul W. Anderson, Ph.D.

New Rules For Relationships and Modern Marriage
Love Is Not Enough

By Paul W. Anderson, Ph.D.

netPsychologist.com Publications
Overland Park, Kansas

If the old rules about how to do marriage and intimate relationships worked, I would be out of business.

But, guess what: I have a thriving business working with couples who want more out of marriage and intimacy than their culture knows how to give them. The American culture pumps people full of high expectations about love relationships. It does not deliver to its citizens on how to achieve that.

Oh sure, kids are born and raised. Mortgages are paid and some way or another we have enough money to do something we might call a vacation. Meanwhile, people who expected partnership, mutual respect and admiration along with the deepening of endearment are disappointed. The high rate of divorce in America is one of the lesser indicators that we really don't know how to do successful marriage.

If you will take the time to read and practice what's in this book, you will see your marriage or partnership relationship differently. You will function differently with your partner both on the levels of communication and intimate interaction and as a result you will gain consequences closer to what you hoped for when you coupled up in the first place.

Love is never enough to do anything you love to do well enough to keep on loving it. It also takes skill, whether it's flying an airplane, making a cake, raising a child or making a marriage work to meet your needs.

Here is your book of relationship skills to guide you into intimate joy with the partner of your choice.

You add the love.

Disclaimer

All the information provided in this book is the property of the Paul W. Anderson, Ph.D. (author), and any publication, in part or as a whole needs to be authorized by him first. The author takes no responsibility for any loss or damage caused due to the misappropriation of this book.

This book is solely for educational purposes and should be read and used as such. This is not a substitution for medical or psychological advice. The author has made all the efforts to provide accurate information and facts, however, any changes in the future are unforeseeable and thus subject to change.

About The Author

How you start something determines where you end up. The "DNA" patterns of a relationship are established in the dating and courtship of a couple. But, people can change the patterns they have been using. Paul W. Anderson, Ph.D. uses his unique counseling approach coupled with the power of special skill building tips and concepts to help couples put joy back in their relationship or marriage and keep it there!

When you need that extra motivation and the insight to use it strategically to achieve your goal, Dr. Anderson can help. Paul Anderson coaches people to get from where they are to where they want to be without giving up who they are.

A licensed psychologist in private practice over 30 years, he has seasoned and fine-tuned his work with couples. Now he shares some of his relationship changing knowledge and skill with you.

Please contact him at 913-901-9110, 843-422-1408

www.netpsychologist.com
www.netpsychologistonline.com

Paul W. Anderson, Ph.D.

Contents

Summary

Marriage is an important institution, and it requires just as much, perhaps even more effort to make it work, as does any other relationship. Nobody gets married knowing or wanting it to end one day. It seemed the relationship was eternal and would last forever when you decided to get married, or when you promised to be together until the "death do us apart." Sadly, the 50% divorce ratio in America is a testament to the fact that something isn't working. A fact that you are reminded about time and again and yet ignore, thinking that you are above it and that you know what it takes to make a marriage work.

It's only when your own marriage seems to be trashed and "on the rocks" that you ponder on why more and more marriages do not seem to be working. You may blame it on the changing times, expectations, lack of love, the infamous "irreconcilable differences" or simply your partner or yourself. For the most part, you may be right. Many things can contribute to marital discord. However, expecting it to work just because "you were meant to be together" or because "you think you understand each other" or (the biggest mis-belief of all time) "you are in love" is wishful thinking. In addition, it is only working half the time.

You do not expect your car to run smoothly without any maintenance or to repair itself automatically if it breaks, do you? Do you go to your local grocery store and expect the lady at the counter to get everything for you because you have been going there for quite some time so she should, by now, be able to read your mind and know exactly what you want?

Unless you're married to somebody with impressive telepathic powers, marriage is no different. The fact is that a marriage, just like any other living organism or non-living object requires maintenance to stay fit and functional.

With a little help from Hollywood movies and other purveyors of mythology, such as fairy tales, movies and novels, in America the primary belief is that the survival of a marriage depends on whether love is still present. Moreover, the whole institution of marriage is left hanging in the air depending on the answer to that question. The fact is that love has

very little to do with making a marriage work or last. The longevity and quality of any relationship depends on the interpersonal skills used by the two main characters, you and your partner.

The reality is that you have the option to ask many questions, put out a little more effort and dig a little deeper before giving up on your relationship. This book will help and guide you in asking those questions of yourself and your partner in order to make sure that you do not let the misguided American beliefs about love and marriage define or destroy your relationship. We need to <u>do</u> and <u>think</u> and <u>feel</u> differently or we will be doing more of the same old broken marriages.

I want to help you explore possibilities and issues that you may not have been able to put your finger on or thought about. You and your partner can fix your relationship without being able to know all the factors that made it anemic. The first thing couples often do when their relationship becomes shaky is to look for something or someone to point a finger at and blame, as if that was the "cause" of the marital trouble.

Here is the first thing I want you to remember: to avoid anger at yourself or another person, to stay away from depression or even self-loathing, the problem in your relationship is not you or your partner. ==It is the patterns of thought and interaction you are using that creates the trouble==, not the people.

Myths and preconceived notions about marriage rob people of the chance to be in the kind of relationship they want and deserve. With a little help and counseling to make strategic changes, you can make sure that you make the most out of your marriage. Joyful intimacy can be a reality for you, but you may need to make a few changes from what your culture, church or society taught you.

Introduction

Some partners act as if their wedding day is the climax to a courtship process that ends in "getting married," as in, "What did you do yesterday?" Answer: "I got married." It is the day when couples assume their understanding of each other, their love and their hard work on the relationship up to the wedding day has paid off. Like a race that has been run and finished, they have arrived at their destination: marriage. They act as if they believe this is the high point after which they can sit back and coast through the rest of their married life.

More often than not, partners assume because they are married and love each other they now have the right to depend on their partners for their emotional support, comfort and happiness. As a society, we may have moved past the ages where the husband was the bread earner and the woman the homemaker, however, as far as emotional dependency goes, not much has changed. We still expect the other person to completely understand and accept all our insecurities and worries. When that doesn't happen, false conclusions can be drawn.

Unrealistic expectations of your partner such as the desire to be understood always without judgment can disrupt the most stable of relationships. Most couples I have worked with agree that quality marriage takes work. Problem is, they don't really know what to specifically work on.

That's my job, to identify and pinpoint the precise behavior(s) and perspective(s) to use to get the results a couple wants.

For example, in the case of wanting to be understood by your partner, the thing to work on is to listen to your partner before expecting them to listen to you. It takes some skill and practice to listen to what your partner wants or is feeling when you have a different opinion. It's even more difficult when you feel misunderstood or not heard by your partner or spouse. However, it can be done and when done properly, this is a great gift of love to your mate.

This book is my guide that shows you how to get a strategic focus that leads to what you want in your marriage. It is the secret to restoring joy to your relationship. A "strategic focus" means working on the right skills and steps that will most ==effectively and efficiently== restore health to a relationship and sustain that relationship quality.

Read "New Rules For Relationships and Modern Marriages" with an open mind, without jumping to conclusions. Consider each possibility and solution I suggest without judgment. Try them out before omitting them as not for you. What you read here is evidence-based, tried and true skill sets and perspectives, which have helped many couples, achieve the intimacy level they want with each other. It is the knowledge base I have used to build my successful marriage counseling practice over the past thirty plus years. Now, I pass what I have learned on to you.

Common Myths and False Assumptions That Can Wreck Marriage
In the past, divorces were less frequent because, as an old traditional couple once put it, "We did not throw away what was broken; we fixed it." Furthermore, historically, there were stronger moral and religious barriers against marital breakup. A person also had to prove to the courts they "deserved" a divorce and that was not always easy.

Today, much of the stigma associated with divorce is gone. In fact, legally, when a marriage legally ends, it is called "dissolution" of a civil contract. If there is a contest over the dissolution, it is about the property settlement and/or the parenting plan, if children are involved.

Suffice it to say, when a relationship or marriage ends, in all likelihood, one or more of the following myths and mis-beliefs have been involved:

Conflict Means It's Over: Just because you are fighting does not mean that the relationship is in a bad phase. Any two individuals living together are bound to have disagreements and different thought processes. You most likely have had disagreements or differences of opinion with your siblings, your parents and even your best friends, but that did not mean those relationships were over. Conflict is human and can actually draw people closer if done properly.

Open and even heated disagreement between love partners can be a healthy part of strengthening a relationship provided the fight is done by the "Rules of Fair Fighting" and there is respect of differing opinions. These Rules are discussed later in more detail (see page 43).

If Only My Partner Loved Me: If only they loved you, what? They could read your mind, they would not upset you, and they would know precisely what you want for Christmas? This one sentence gets couples into deep trouble because, unless they talk to each other, what each person needs and wants will never be known to each other. Moreover, it presumes your partner will show their love for you the same way you do. Usually, that is not the case. They are different from you.

If you expect that loving each other means your partner understands exactly how you feel and what you want without talking with them, when that doesn't happen you take it as a sign of lack of love.

You can be insanely in love and may have known each other a long time, but that does not guarantee your mate will know you want to go away for a romantic weekend to the Bahamas just because you said you were tired. Just because you have to vocalize about the things you need/want does not mean love is gone.

Putting Yourself First in Marriage is Selfish: Once you are married, the focus of the relationship may change from "me" and "you" to "we" and "us". However, getting married does not mean you aren't an individual any longer with personal and separate needs from your spouse.

A healthy relationship requires two healthy individuals, and in order to be healthy, you will need to take care of yourself first and heed to your desires and needs even more so. That will keep you in good shape so you can be a solid contributor to the relationship. The healthy model for a durable relationship is two people taking good care of themselves in each other's presence, and as they do that, they take their partner's needs into account, as well.

True "Love" Relationships Don't Need Help: This is one stigma that just doesn't seem to go away. Acknowledging the fact that your relationship might need help is difficult because according to general beliefs, it means accepting that you are failing. However, nothing could be further from the truth. A willingness to seek professional help indicates that you value your relationship and are willing to take good care of it. You take your car in for service, don't you? You get your hair done regularly, the dog groomed and the kids teeth checked. How is your marriage any different?

A professional marriage counselor cannot make you fall in love with your partner again, or decide whether you belong together or not. He or she can help you understand and realize potential problems, provide possible solutions and help keep a healthy communication flow between the two of you. Marriage counseling is as important as regular visits to the dentist, or the automobile garage..

Unanswered Questions That Prevent Couples Knowing Who They Really Married

Communication is the key to any healthy relationship; it is only through open and honest communication that you can sustain a relationship. However, this does not always mean proclamation of love or sharing a joke. A healthy, communicative relationship is just as much about telling the person what you like about them, as it is about expressing what you dislike.

Some individuals keep their feelings and opinions suppressed so as to avoid awkward confrontations. However, long term, these can pile up and negatively affect the relationship.

It's better to know your partner, both what you like and don't like about them. They are not your clone. How boring that would be! Furthermore, samey-samey, total agreement about everything, big and small, is not the key to strong relationships.

Following are some questions every couple needs to ask in order to see if they are have enough compatibility to suit them:

1. What are your goals or mission statement as a couple?
2. To what medical lengths are you willing to go to have children?
3. Can you name two real-life couples you admire and want to be like?
4. If your child has severe disabilities, what would you do to care for them?
5. After 10 years of marriage, what will the sex life be like and what will you be willing to do to keep it vibrant?
6. Will you share your credit reports with each other before you marry and after?
7. If one or both of you want out of the marriage, how will you handle that?
8. What did you learn from you previous relationships that will help your current relationship be healthy?
9. How do you handle conflict and does it fit with the other's style?
10. Is there something in your history, legally, medically or otherwise you would not want me to know about?

These questions may seem unromantic, or perhaps even harsh. However, these kind of questions can help you know more clearly who you are involved with.

The deal here is to know what you are getting into with the person you have partnered with or plan to. Differences in and of themselves are not deal breakers, but knowing this kind of information about your partner can avoid big wake-up calls in the future and give you a chance to find compromises sooner than later.

Many individuals also avoid asking these questions because they believe it would hinder their relationship. The reality is that you may fear the answers to these questions, and the fact that they may not be what you hope and pray for. Hence, the fear of knowing the truth or being bitten by the harsh reality of life prompts you to delay asking such questions. However, you then run the risk of finding out the answers the harsher way. By then, it may be too late.

Common Phrases That Create Trouble in a Relationship

You may believe that your partner has been behaving unseemly as of late, and is probably showing his "true colors" or is "not in his senses," but the fact is that there are some common patterns between most troubled couples.

"You Have Changed"

"You have changed. You're not who I married." Often I hear this in a relationship that has aged a few years. When I ask when the change first started, it is frequently traced back to either after the wedding or after the first child was born.

Maybe, as stated earlier, you didn't make efforts to fully know the person you were getting married to. Now, some hidden traits are showing up and your mates seems different, as the result.

But, people do change and for legitimate reasons, not because they hid a part of themselves from you. They grow up and mature. Tragedy happens. Partners have life experiences that change them. That is not the problem. Not keeping up with each other on a regular basis is the problem.

"I am the Problem"

Being married is a special bond, but it is not the only thing that defines you. Every time your partner is upset or angry or frustrated does not mean you are the cause behind it. The pressures in the American society to make a marriage work "no matter what" is so strong that partners, for fear of failing, start taking each issue and problem personally. Sure, you have your part in whatever happens in a relationship, but it is unrealistic to hog all the blame.

The truth about human emotion: each of us is responsible for what we feel and do. Feelings are based on perceptions and perceptions are based on our thoughts. We are able and responsible to manage our feelings by managing perceptions and thoughts. In turn, we are able to manage our behaviors.

Here are a few more phrases based on falsehoods that can trouble intimate partnerships:

- "I don't want to hurt your feelings."
- "You should know how that makes me feel!"
- "You should have said "Sorry' first because you started it."
- "You don't love me anymore."
- "We don't have time."
- "I don't want to talk about it."
- "I'm leaving. I knew this marriage wouldn't work."

Tip: Most problematic phrases have many "you" words in them. Also, there are often absolute words such "never" or "always" or controlling words like "should" or "selfish."

Phrases such as these can feel like personal attacks and then the fight begins, again. Not good.

Chapter 1
Why the Relationship Isn't Working?

Statistics show that an American couple has a 50-50 chance of getting past the third year in marriage and a 50-50 chance of getting divorced between the 18th and 25th year of marriage if you survive the first three years. These statistics are not pretty, but if you are going to do something different with your marriage than has been given to you from your culture and the American society, I think we have to look past the "usual suspects', such as individual fault or the absence of love as the root cause. I suggest instead, we focus on the patterns of thought and behavior, false perceptions and unrealistic expectations the couple uses that don't work.

It is mistaken to believe that people in other cultures where the break-up rate of significant relationships is lower than ours, love more truly or produce better human beings than we Americans do. In fact, many societies which produce long term, solid relationships marry for reasons other than love.

Marriage is no different from another human relationship. If you have ever shared quarters with another individual or even shared a room with your sibling, you know that when personalities clash there are bound to be differences. Unless you haven't married a clone who feels what you feel, who eats what you eat, showers as regularly as you shower, is happy when you are happy and is sad when you are sad, chances are there will be differences between you and your mate.

We go at marriage and intimate relationships with different patterns than we do our friendships, work relationships and even other family relationship like those between parent and child or siblings. And that's what makes the difference.

What keeps your marriage from working the way you want it to? Here are some of the reasons I know about, patterns of thinking and expectations that don't work very well to produce quality marriages or relationships.

The Perfect Life

Speak to any individual who has tried to apply all the secrets of leading a perfect life and he or she will tell you there is no such thing as a perfect life. Well, that is just the reality. The idea of a perfect married life is equally a lie we like to believe in. Pop culture and our obsession with "love" make us vulnerable to thinking this is attainable.

As humans, we are tempted to compare our lives with others, people who have a better car, a better house, and in general better living style and relationships than others. That comparison can "make" us feel bad.

Using the same reasoning, if you want to feel better, you just have to find people leading a poorer quality of life than yourself and compare your life to them.

But this is not a healthy practice. How Warren Buffett amassed his money may inspire you. Hard work, determination and financial intelligence are skills worth using, but they should be desired as good values in and of themselves, not because a rich man you admire uses them.

Similarly, it is not healthy to envy other people's relationships. Just because your sister's best friend's husband leaves love notes to his wife on the refrigerator does not mean you should necessarily do the same. Use your own ways and means to foster romance and solid connections for you and your mate because they work for you, not because you want to be like someone else.

True, someone else's behavior may give you an idea to use. But, perhaps funny pictures or political cartoons on the frig will work better for you and your beloved than love letters. An idea is only as good as the good results it produces in your life, in your relationship.

Society's Pressure

No one wants to admit that their relationship is failing. How is it that you can tell your neighbor that you had an argument with your brother and haven not spoken since, but it's difficult to admit you had a disagreement with your husband or wife?

I think it is because society sees a failed or troubled relationship with your spouse as a negative reflection on you as a person. But, if you and a friend argue and have trouble, for some goofy reason, that seems not so bad or worrisome. Not to say trouble in other relationships is of no concern, but it doesn't seem to carry the societal stigma that trouble between intimate partners does in our society. That puts unnecessary pressure on marriage.

Whose Fault is it?

No relationship is complete without an occasional brawl over who is right and who's at fault. Extended blame games, however, can be a never ending charade which seldom leads to mending relationships. When you start blaming your partner for relationship troubles, you block free and fair communication. When blamed, we get defensive. Problems are not solved as a team when members of the team are divided by the poison of blame.

Anyway, remember, it is not one person's fault or responsibility to take the burden of the entire relationship. Placing all the blame on one person hinders relationship development. In most cases, you will have a part in the trouble. Focus on that because you can change you.

You can't change your partner. Focus on your partner's faults only grinds things down into painful paralysis.

Expectations

Being married is a change of identity. Your duties and your priorities change, and so do your expectations. You may believe that because you are madly in love with your partner and because your partner is in love with you, everything is going to be perfect. You expect the other to understand your mood swings, your dreams, your needs, your habits and your insecurities and to heed them one by one, without providing any "instructions" or the need to say anything.

That is not possible between humans. Every relationship is based on give and take, whether it is the materialistic things, physical pleasures, exchange of ideas or expressing what you desire from a relationship. Give and take expectations have to be experimented with and learned. Each couple will find their own "quid pro quo" and develop their own realistic expectations.

How Your Family Affects Your Relationship Or Marriage

This may come as a surprise to you. In a world where families hardly ever intervene in the personal matters of a married couple, it is hard to believe that family actually has an influence on what you look for in a relationship. Your family actually helped pick the person you fell in love with. Sure, we're usually not conscious of how the dynamics of our family's origin strongly influence the "love" choices that we make. However, here are some of the major family patterns which influence who you choose as your life partner:

Family Loyalty

If you grew up eating with a fork and knife then the chances are you wouldn't choose someone who only eats with their fingers or if you were scolded for biting your nails as a child then you may not feel too comfortable being around someone who still bites nails or cracks knuckles. Other patterns like ethnicity, socio-economic status, religious beliefs, quality of life and chronic anxiety all stay with us and influence our likes and preferences. We show loyalty to our family by imitating them, even when we may think we're doing the opposite.

A client once told she worked very hard to not be like her parents. They had been very dogmatic with her as a child, insisting things were either right or wrong. As she matured, she can to realize there are gray areas to life and things are not always so clearly black or white.

So now, as a parent she old me, she *insists* that her children understand there are grey areas in life. It occurred to me as she talked that she was being loyal to her parents by being just as dogmatic as her parents had been, albeit, about a different issue.

Reciprocity

If you were a bossy sibling, chances are you'd like a partner who doesn't boss you back. Likewise, if in your family of origin you were in the habit of making breakfast for your siblings, helping them out with homework, and saw to it that things got organized in the home, someone who likes being taken care of and directed would be very interested in you as a mate.

It's difficult to have two expert planners in one house, or two bad listeners, or two leaders or even two followers. Patterns of behavior in one mate need to fit those in the other partner. Otherwise, the discord will end the dating before the relationship has a chance to even get started.

Emotional Familiarity

One of the most common ways people determine if they are compatible with the other person is if they feel comfortable around them. During courtship, you try not to speak too much about your true feelings, likes and dislikes and lifestyle. However, as you start getting comfortable with the other person, you start telling them about all those intimate and at times, not so rosy personal details. If the other person "understands" you and your personality and you feel you are comfortable talking about anything with him or her, you may feel you have found "the one."

However, rather than looking for the comfort factor, what you are actually responding to is familiarity. Comfort is mostly based on familiarity. Perhaps more unconsciously than not, we quickly sense if the person we are interested in behaves with emotional patterns we know and have experienced before. That's OK if those patterns we are familiar with are good for us. If you keep dating this person, you are setting up to repeat your emotional and relationship history. Hopefully, that history is a good one for you to repeat. If not, the irony is you best be dating someone you don't feel so comfortable with

We seldom date, let alone court, a person we don't feel comfortable or familiar with.

Power Struggles in Finances

It is safe to say that finances play a major role in making or breaking the quality of relationship. We live in a culture where money equals power

and whether we like it or not, couples can destabilize their relationship if they mismanage money and the power it represents.

For instance, one partner might feel that since they earn more money than their mate, they should have control over the finances and purchases. At the same time, the person who makes little or no money may feel controlled by their partner who "owns" all the money because they make more. This can lead to conflict and resentments.

The best solution I know of for equality in money/power management is for the couple to have three different checking accounts, one each for both the partners and third one a joint account for household expenditures.

Each person then is responsible to deposit into the joint account their percentage of the joint bills based on the percent of income they each provide to the household. Once this responsibility to the joint account has been met, the partners are free to use the remaining money in their accounts as they fit, unencumbered by the other partner.

Even in cases where only one person is earning, I strongly advise couples to keep three accounts, two for personal allowances and the third for household expenditures, funding the one personal account that has no income with an allowance that is part of the joint expense budget.

Chapter 2
Digging Deeper:
More Sources of Trouble and Solution Tips

You probably related to at least some of the problems discussed in Chapter I. At some point, all relationships go through difficulties. The trick is to work together to find solutions as opposed to attacking each other as if your partner is the source of the trouble.

Armed with insight and a better understanding of each other and how relationships work, a couple can find ways to compromise, build bridges between their differences and mature their relationship with quality.

Here are some of the core reasons behind some of the most common issues that couples face in today's modern times:

When Love is "Gone" (Or So It Seems)
What we call love comes from choice, behavior and feeling. Couples who worry that love is gone often have forgotten how love came in the first place. They forget that they made choices with each other to behave or act in particular ways that we called dating and/or courtship. He says, "Let's go on a date." She says, "Great. Pick me up at eight," or something like that.

Decisions and choice like these make dating or just hanging out with each other become reality.

As a couple does and says certain things to each other, feelings can begin to emerge between them. The point here is that the solid emotional attachment toward somebody else that we call "love" comes after action and behavior, not before. I have seen couples who thought love was gone, restore those loving feelings by remembering and doing what they did in the first place that led to love.

A popular book by the title, "Talk To Me Like I'm Someone You Love," (see References) is made up of flash cards that a couple can turn to and use to remind themselves that acting and talking in loving ways has benefit, even if you don't feel so loving at the time.

Despite the fact that "love is not enough" to make a relationship work over time, it certainly can grease the skids, as it were, and make things a little easier. However, we have to do "it" before we feel "it." All of us have that capacity to use will power to make the choice to do something we don't feel like doing. We go to work when we don't feel like it. You take care of your child giving him or her what they need whether you feel like it or not. Likewise, there is value in talking and treating your spouse lovingly at times when you don't feel like it (tough as that may be).

Those sweet gestures of love have value. No matter the depth of trouble in a relationship, things are never 100% bad, even though they may feel that way momentarily. Every relationship has some good to it. Every partner has a loveable side. It's good to remember that and act accordingly. Feelings can be very powerful, both positively and negatively and influence behavior. It is also true that feelings will follow behavior, that acting the way you want to feel can lead to actually having those feelings.

Each person is in charge of their own feelings. You may want to blame your partner for the way you feel, but truth be told, your feelings come out of your perceptions and expectations. You can shape your perceptions with your behavior. Next time you're in a fight with someone, give it a try. Act toward them as if you loved them and cared for them and can't possibly see yourself going through life without them. See if that can have a good effect on your feelings. "Faking It 'till You Make It" has value.

Body Language

At times even the smallest body gestures can lead to bigger problems. Paying attention to your nails when the other is talking or staring at the walls, shrugging shoulders, frowning, rolling eyes, or smirking, all these can be misconstrued as disrespecting and hurtful.

Nonverbal communications are often even more powerful than our words. A well-timed eye roll can set up the stage for the next nuclear war between a couple more quickly than being called dozens of the worst names imaginable.

During counseling sessions I hear couples say things like, "He looked at me that way," or "She was watching TV while I was talk and didn't hear a thing I said," and they tell me that's when the fight started.

When things are good between a couple, they take it for granted. However, the same dynamics are at play as when things turn sour. When the couple is getting along well with each other they are speaking and acting out kinder, more cooperative and caring signals to each other. It's just that when there is no trouble you don't pay attention to those subtleties in body language.

Be aware of what message your partner may be getting from your body language. This can have as much, and sometimes more of an impact, on your communications with your partner as what you say with verbal language.

Most importantly, be sure you are honest and do not send one message with your body and a contradictory message with your words. Double messages will start fights.

When Similar Personalities Clash

Although it is fun and exciting to be with someone who has similar interests or similar taste in films, music, books, etc., it can be quite difficult to be with someone who has a similar personality. For instance, if you are introverted, then being with someone who is just as shy or reserved may halter the communication flow.

The basic reason behind similar personalities crashing is that they both have the same strengths, but also the same weaknesses. For instance, if both partners are cleanliness freaks, it may be great, because then the house would always be in order. However, competition between the couple can arise as to who cleaned the house better or the right way.

If you find yourself having what is sometimes called "personality differences" between you and your partner, it's a good time to go back and check out what initially, even in your dating, helped you to feel comfortable with your partner.

Familiar traits and characteristics can attract us because we know them and understand them. They can also be the things we complain about in our partner for a variety of reasons. For example, if we don't like certain traits or behaviors in ourselves, we may criticize them in our partner. We can see them more clearly in our partner than we can in ourselves and so the conflict starts again when we try to change them.

Whatever the reason for the personality clashes, the couple is still challenged with this source of conflict, as with any kind of conflict, to find solutions together as a team, rather than trying to change each other.

Denial

No problem or disease is too small to ignore. This is certainly true in relationships. You may believe an unresolved argument or problem will eventually be forgotten, but that is seldom the case. These small glitches or irritants mount up and lead to resentment, anger, alienation and acting out behaviors.

If there is a problem, no matter how small, make sure you do not ignore it. Talk about it. Every time you say to yourself "It's nothing," at least discuss "the nothing" with your partner. If indeed it is nothing, then there's nothing to worry about. In the meantime, you've at least reached out and made a connection with your partner. If there is a problem, hopefully you can deal with it better as a couple, not a lonely burden to bear by yourself.

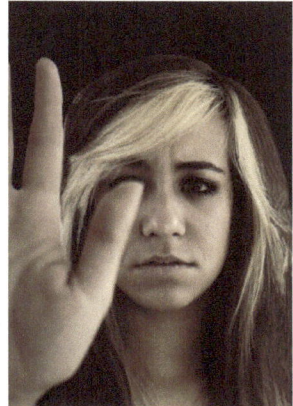

Some people feel things are OK in a relationship if there is less talking. Other's feel just the opposite and silence is a signal of trouble. It's amazing how often these two opposites marry each other. Both need to learn how to be a little more like their mate and meet in the middle: more talking for the one and a little less for the other.

Discussions between couples that put critical issues on the table certainly need to be handled with tact and healthy communication procedures. The guidelines here can help a couple tread through emotional land mine fields safely and find resolution to problems:

- Use "I" statements. Avoid "you" statements.
- Own the concern as your own.
- Do not criticize, judge or blame.
- Be willing to set a date to talk about your concern and agree on a place both you and your partner will feel safe to talk undisturbed.
- Don't ambush each other with a sudden blast of verbiage about a hot topic. Be deliberate, set up the arrangements, then dialogue.

If there is any one single thing I recommend to couples as they go through difficult times it is to keep the dialogue going. No matter what, keep talking.

Fear

Some topics are fearful to discuss, such as, "Is our marriage over?" or "Are you having an affair?" You may not even want to acknowledge small problems for fear of making things worse. This increasing fear of failing and avoidance of concerns can bring about the very thing you fear.

NO RELATIONSHIP IS EVER A WASTE OF YOUR TIME. IF IT DIDN'T BRING YOU WHAT YOU WANT, IT TAUGHT YOU WHAT YOU DON'T WANT.

It's better to talk about your fears with your spouse than incubate them in silence until they breed and become reality. This can be a good time to have a third-party present such as a counselor or coach to help you broach difficult or toxic topics.

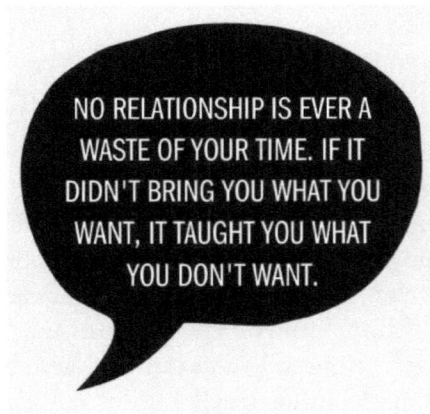

You Only Get Married Once

You only want to get married once when you want to get married. This stereotypical thinking that you are only supposed to get married once, has led people to try too hard to stay married rather than stay happy and act in loving ways to each other. There are worse things than a relationship that didn't work out the way you initially dreamed it would.

Research shows that an addict has a 90% chance of a relapse as they work toward sobriety and recovery. But, no one judges an addict when he or she has a slip. The reasoning is that they are trying and even in relapse, can learn things that will eventually strengthen recovery.

But, when a marriage fails, society starts pointing fingers. Yes, I encourage you to do all you can to save your relationship and to make it work. But, do so only because that's what you want to do, not because you're trying to avoid shame or embarrassment. You are free to try marriage and find ways to make it work for you as many times as you need to.

Wedding vows often include the phrase, "'till death do us part" or something similar. Generally, we think of this as a reference to physical death of one of the partners. However, relationships also can die spiritual, emotional or social deaths. If you believe that your relationship has died, try resuscitation, if that makes sense to you. On the other hand, I think it's better to be in touch with reality than to pretend otherwise and stay in a dead relationship.

Unforgiving Attitudes

Bernard Meltzer (host to the radio show, "What's Your Problem?") said, "When you forgive, you in no way change the past, but you sure do change the future." Couples can and do give each other another chance even after having made mistakes. They can forgive each other.

What isn't helpful is bringing up the past in present fights. Most people's memory works well especially when they've been burned or hurt by the behavior of an intimate partner. However, if you choose to stay with your partner and work through a rough patch such as infidelity, physical abuse or substance abuse, reminding your partner later on of those difficult times when he or she let you down is a sign of being stuck in the past you thought you were past.

Modern marriages are volitional, meaning they are a matter of choice between consenting adults. We don't have to be married or have a partner in order to make it through life like people once did in this society.

Some people are honest enough with themselves and their partner to declare they are not able to live with certain circumstances, such as cheating. If that's the case for you, act accordingly and yes, during transitioning out of that relationship there will be some difficulty.

In the long run, leaving a marriage and making those adjustments will not be nearly as destructive to the quality of your life, that of your children or even your partner, as staying married, but continuing to live in memory of painful times past.

If you're stuck and you choose to stay in the marriage, do anything and everything you can to not constantly remind the other person of their mistakes. Nothing is gained by continue to remind your mate of their shortcomings, past or present.

Oh and by the way, whether or not you want to admit it, you had a part in bringing about your spouse's failing. Find out what it is even if it takes professional counseling to do that. Say and mean, "I'm sorry." Then, with or without that partner, get on with your life.

Tip: If you can live with your partner the way they are now, things in the marriage can work. If, however, you want them different in some way and that difference preoccupies you, regularly bothers you and is a frequent focus of your feelings and thoughts, that for me is a red flag you best not ignore.

Wishing your partner was the way you knew them to be when you married may be worth a nostalgic thought or two, but be careful. Do not try to change them. Rather, find ways to make the benefits of being in the relationship worth the cost or pain so you can live well with this partner. If that is not possible, even with the help of counseling, give thought to other options.

Chapter 3
What May Be Holding Your Relationship Back?

Here are few more things to consider that can hinder the growth and the development of quality in an intimate, ongoing relationship. Not only the inter-active dynamics between a couple can affect what happens to a marriage, but a marriage can be only as healthy as the two partners involved. The following are some red flags for you personally to consider.

Exhaustion

Eventually your married life becomes monotonous. There is nothing new left to experience, or so it seems. Our brains need stimulation or we become bored. Left to the unconscious to solve this problem and find stimulation, couples may fight or get the kids overly scheduled with activities or go into debt or build a house....anything to give themselves something to focus on.

Our focus can turn to work, an affair, neighborhood projects, etc. almost anything will do once your relationship no longer captures your curiosity and interest. Eventually, the marriage or relationship becomes so matter-of-fact and uninteresting you don't even want to put out any effort to make things better.

Relationship exhaustion can result in couples getting more and more distant without realizing it until they become no more than two strangers living under the same roof.

This doesn't have to happen if you're mindful about this pitfall and make deliberate and conscious efforts to keep yourself interesting to your partner. Stay curious about your partner rather than controlling of them. And through it all, talk, talk, talk. Even if all you have to talk about is relationship exhaustion and boredom, talk about that.

Mind Reading and Assumptions

The most skilled of doctors will not try to read your mind about what is ailing you. Instead, they ask you numerous questions, run tests and thoroughly examine you. Then, they base their diagnose on all that information. When a medical person uses this approach, you do not question his or her abilities or skills to cure the disease. In fact, if the doctor used mind reading, you would certainly question their competence.

If your partner is angry or exhausted, don't use mind reading and jumping to unfounded conclusion with them. Get some facts from your loved one before assuming they are upset with something about you. If he comes home not too happy, that does not automatically mean he is happier away from home.

Keep an open mind about things and don't jump to conclusions without factual information. Even if you are having a fight or an argument, make sure that you are listening with an open mind, rather than only believing what you want to believe as if you can read your partner's mind.

Tips:

- Don't finish your loved one's sentences
- Don't walk away or tune out in between explanations or change the subject just because you think you've heard it before
- If it is not what you wanted to hear, listen even more attentively.

Pre-judging and jumping to conclusions before the facts come out will negatively affect healthy conversation. Head off bigger problems by gathering facts about what is going on with your partner rather than trying to read their mind.

If indeed the facts prove your mind reading was right, you will have the documentation to validate your clairvoyance!

Saying "Yes" When You Need to Say "No"

"No" is one of the most powerful words in the dictionary. Unfortunately, not many people realize its power. "No" is the only protection we have against boundary violation and giving self away to the point where there's nothing of you left.

"Yes" may be good, but "No" at the right time can be better. The thing is, if you say yes to everything, it becomes a default setting, without much meaning. Few people want a spineless "Yes" person for a partner. If you can say, "No" when you need to, saying "Yes" will have a ring of truth and value to it.

Knowing when to say "yes" or "no" requires brutal honesty with yourself and your partner. Of course, tact and courtesy are essential. In the long run, nothing good comes out of exhausting yourself trying to please everyone around you. You may believe you are being a good wife, a good mother or a good friend. Yet, how would you feel if your son started doing everything that his siblings, his friends or classmates asked him to do? Chances are you wouldn't like it or think it was healthy for him.

Doing everything the others ask or expect you to do is not only exhausting, but sooner or later will result in you losing your individuality. If you don't want to go out for dinner or a movie, for example, or don't feel like cooking, just say so. It doesn't make you a bad anything, just a human being with normal feelings, emotions and changes of mood.

If your partner has other desires, that is a good time to negotiate a compromise. A compromise will give each of you a little of what you need but probably not everything. Marriages that know how to compromise in fair and equal ways are much more likely to be viable, long-term relationships.

Even if you aren't comfortable saying "No" directly, then answers like, "Let me think about it," or "I'll get back to you about it", or "I am not too comfortable about that," can be very helpful. Practice using "No" as a tool for self-differentiation before others start taking you for granted as a "Yes person."

Ego

Father doesn't always know best and as a rule modern couples understand that "My Way or the Highway" doesn't work very well in the long run. Ego, pride, the inability to be influenced by others or negotiate compromises can certainly ruin the quality of a marriage or intimate relationship.

The research of many psychologists concludes that America has reaped a bumper crop of narcissists in the last three decades. The characteristic of the narcissistic personality most damaging to relationship quality is the inability of this person to put themselves in the shoes of their partner. With no ability for empathy, authentic emotional intimacy is not possible.

Living with a self-centered partner may leave you feeling frustrated, desperate and hopeless. Do all the research you can about narcissism so that you understand it as a disease. That information will also help you take better care of yourself and make good decisions about your marriage. You may also find benefit working with a counselor.

Expectations

I have already commented on the negative effects unrealistic interpersonal expectations can have on a relationship, for example with regard to the over importance of what is call "being in love". The same holds true for unrealistic expectations about personal behavior and performance.

Striving to be super mom, to do and be everything for everybody not only leads to personal depletion, but it can get in the way of being present to healthy, balanced functioning in your marriage. The house does not always have to be so clean or the dishes done just so. Even if you have to arrange for childcare and be away from the kids awhile, it's worth it if you can get some time out periodically with your partner or friends to keep your needs met.

Some men carry unrealistic expectations about monetary earnings, or sexual performance that leads to unnecessary anxiety. Performance anxiety for either men or women reaches a point of diminishing returns and takes from the relationship instead of adding to it.

The rule of the Golden Mean or keeping a healthy balance between not too much and not too little of anything is a good guideline for personal, as well as relationship behavior.

No, You Are Not All of a Sudden in Love with Your Neighbor

But, it may look that way to your partner. Just because your relationship is on the rocks and you have found a shoulder to lean on does not mean you have fallen out of love with your mate and in love with another person. It may only mean that someone has lent you an ear when you needed to talk. Maybe you simply want to be with someone with whom you have less tension.

During times when we are emotionally frayed and upset, we can be vulnerable to unintended consequences, especially if the ear we choose to share our troubles with belongs to a person of the opposite sex. Emotional affairs are easy to slide into and of course any kind of extramarital intimacy will only add to the difficulties your marriage or relationship may already be dealing with.

There's nothing wrong with finding a sounding board to vent and process your thoughts and feelings. But, leaning on the beautiful or handsome neighbor of the opposite sex (assuming you are heterosexual) may not serve your marriage in the long run as well as a same-sex confidant could, or better yet a professional counselor.

Getting support is one thing. Flirting with temptation is another. You can be sure, your partner will know the difference, especially if there is trouble already in the relationship.

Chapter 4
How Can These Problems Be Fixed?

Point of Clarification

Relationships are not like flat tires or broken water pipes that can be fixed. With things that don't work right, we find the problem, apply a solution and magically it as if things are back to what is called "normal."

Marriages and intimate couplings, however, are organic in nature. They are living entities, not things. It takes a shift in thinking to approach a wounded relationship with the proper attitude. Yes, changes in thinking and behavior certainly lead to an improvement in a marriage. These changes are shifts in your functioning that have to be, not only started, but sustained. If you nurture these new ways, they will grow and mature, like any living thing that is fed and nurtured.

Relationships, as living entities, have lifespans. They begin, have a midlife and eventually one way or the other, end. While living, they can manifest varying degrees of health. That level of health is dependent upon how well they're regularly taken care of, not a simple matter of "fixing-it" as with a tire when the nail is pulled out, patched and you go on your way without thinking about the tire anymore.

As a marriage counselor, I'm mystified how common it is for people to categorize a relationship as if it were a thing. Having said that, it might be all right to think of your marriage as a thing so long as you tended to its needs with the same mindfulness and regularity some people do with their German engineered cars.

Even so, your marriage is more like your child, your houseplants, your children's goldfish or your garden in the backyard. These are organic, growing entities that must be nurtured or they wither and eventually die. Daily attention, feeding, properly applied TLC and dialogue with your child you do without question. What makes you think your marriage is any different and can survive on leftovers whenever you and your partner get around to it or feel like it?

Once married, the American mind puts marriage last. The dismal harvest we reap with regard to relationships we say are important is no accident.

Don't Give Up

Your marriage will only be over when you think it's over, and if you are in a bad place, you may just need to give it a break. There is absolutely nothing wrong with asking for some space. Rather than giving up on a relationship, an option is to take a break for a specified period of time, such as 30 to 60 days.

This doesn't mean you move out or separate. It can mean the two of you agree to stop trying to fix things and take a break. You may simply be exhausted from trying so hard. Exhausted people often don't think clearly and repeat what has been repeated, expecting different outcomes.

If you use this option, it's important to get back with each other at the end of the timeout period and review/evaluate where you are with each other now. Sometimes, after a cooling off period, partner's brains work better at problem solving and solutions previously unseen become possible.

Use New Imagination, Not New Partners

If you feel your relationship is losing its former glory, then you have the responsibility to do something different as much as your partner does.

Using your imagination to try something different in a given area of your relationship can be as exciting as finding a new partner. Add a new wrinkle to your date night, such as rotating each of you arranging something new and surprising to get out of the old ruts.

Get the book, "The Joy of Sex" (see References) which uses a cookbook approach to physicality. Plan new bedroom delights starting with appetizer, main course and desserts. Go to a different church. Jump into a different social circle. Sit in different places at the family meal table. Start a hobby together. Use your imagination.

Don't Involve Any One Else, Unless It Is a Professional

You may be in the habit of consulting a parent or sibling when things go bad, or perhaps your best friend. But, once you are married, you should lean on your partner to fix things up. Don't call your dad if the sinks break down, or your sister to ask what to get your boss for a birthday. Rather, first seek your partner's advice and expertise and tackle problems together, especially if they pertain to your relationship.

The critical thing to keep in mind here is to avoid triangulation. Triangulation is the process of talking to one person about another person who is not present. The person not present can feel ganged up on. If the person not present happens to be your spouse, they will get defensive if they find out you've talked about them behind their back.

Perhaps the sink does need to be fixed and it is possible your husband or partner does not know the first thing about plumbing. Nevertheless, talk to your partner first about possible solutions or others you may want to get involved in the fix-it process. Then, call the plumber, or your father-in-law for help, if that's what you and your partner have agreed on.

The last thing you want to do is call your father asking for help while at the same time commenting on how inadequate your husband is at plumbing. Things can get even worse if what you're talking to someone else about is how bad your partner is doing something in the relationship. Best policy is to talk first to your partner about whatever the problem may be; getting the grass cut, having more sex or enhancing emotional intimacy through better communication.

Magic Words to Use

Here are some words and phrases you can use to revive your marriage. It may seem like child's play, but if you've ever seen your wife's mood lift because you told her she looks beautiful, or you let your husband know that you do not want to live without him, you will know that words can really make a difference.

Sometimes the effect can seem magical. It's always worth giving the following words a chance to work:

- I love you!
- Remember when…(name something good that happened).
- I'm proud of you.

- You are so clever!
- What can I do to help you?
- You are so special to me!
- I'm sorry. Please forgive me.
- Thank you.
- What are your thoughts about what would be fun to do?
- Please.
- I'm listening.
- I'm here for you.
- I missed you today.
- What are your hopes and dreams about our future together?
- Please forgive me. (Yes, I know I've mentioned this repeatedly and so should you with your partner).

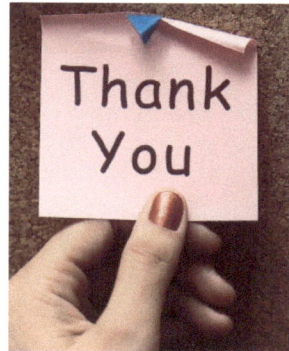

Make Vows One Day At A Time, Not For A Lifetime

Just saying your vows on your wedding day isn't enough. What has to happen is for each person to turn their vows and intentions into daily actions. These actions are not contingent upon your partner's behaviors or how you feel that particular day any more than the job you do for money depends upon whether you feel like it or not. You simply do what is expected of you because it's your job, in this case, the job of loving "husband" or caring "wife."

This may not seem romantic or fit our American expectations of love. But there are lessons for us to learn from cultures where marriages are arranged. In these societies, people do as they are told to do, either as husband or wife. In those spousal roles they perform their duties first. We Westerners do it backwards in that we say if we don't love one another, why would want to do loving husband or caring wife jobs?

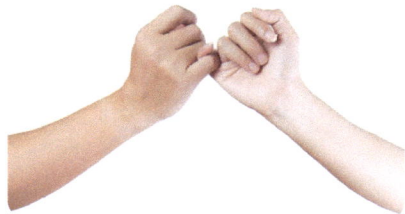

Interestingly enough, however, when anthropologists interview spouses who've been doing their "jobs" with each other over several years, these people declare the fondness and all the feelings for each other we associate with being in love. And the bonus here is that these societies have nominal break-up or divorce rates.

Here are my suggestions for daily spousal pledges or vows:

What the Husband Should Pledge to Make the Marriage Work

"I will be a good husband and do the things a loving husband does, such as share myself emotionally with you, make sure I touch you with affection on a consistent basis and have regular kind interaction with you. I will do these things to show how much I want and respect you, because that is my job to attend to you, my wife, no matter what you do or don't do or how I feel towards you."

What the Wife Should Pledge to Make the Marriage Work

"I will do my job of being a caring wife to you. I will admire you, compliment you, not criticize you (especially in front of others or our children) and be there for you whenever you will need me, physically and emotionally. I will stay be by your side, no matter what you do or don't do or how I feel toward you because that is my job as wife."

Promises like these, constant compliments and sweet gestures can retain the richness in your relationship.

The Pay-Off: Not only do you get the benefit and satisfaction of doing your job well, but when each spouse does their job well, it makes it easier for the other one to do their job well. This can escalate positively to the point of marital bliss.

Tips and Tricks to Communicate Effectively
Myths like the Earth was flat and that the sun revolved around the Earth were finally put to rest with the help of extensive research and scientific evidences. Sadly, many myths about marriage have yet to be put to rest. They continue to plague our society and eat away at relationships.

The trick to making your marriage work and stay healthy is not based on how much you love the other, or how many times a month you eat out or how many holidays you take each year. Marriage takes more than that, a lot more. Following are some of the tips and tricks that are essential in making a marriage work.

Keep an Open Mind: Don't judge or jump to conclusions when having an argument or fighting. Check out your suspicion before you turn it into an accusation. Make sure you think before you say anything, especially if it is an emotional reaction.

Use Active Listening and Feedback Techniques: When talking about household issues, or other personal, social or work related issues that your spouse may be having, make sure to lend a full ear. Say something like "What I hear you saying is…" or "Do you mean to say…?" and repeat what you heard the other say. If you got it right, your partner affirms that. If not, necessary corrections/clarifications are made by your partner and again you feed it back until the message sent is the message received.

This ensures that partners hear each other correctly. "Active listening" is especially useful to avoid misunderstandings when talking about personal and sensitive topics or matters of disagreement. Most people want to be heard more than agreed with.

Rule of thumb is to make sure your partner knows you've heard what they're saying, thinking and feeling before you try to get them to hear you. Listening has nothing to do with whether you agree or not with what the speaker is saying. It simply means, "Yes, I think I've heard you say… . Is that correct?" Once you get affirmation that you received the proper message, then the process is reversed and it is your partners turn to listen to you.

Caution: Don't try to send your message/thoughts/feelings before it's your turn to talk about yourself! Until then, you are only and all ears on what your partner is saying.

Listening means receiving the accurate message the speaker intended to send. Sometimes it takes additional clarification to make sure this is happening. Speakers do not always clearly communicate and you as a listener feeding back what you think has been said can help your partner clarify their message.

The Right Body Language: Make sure your non-verbal gestures don't send off the wrong signals. Try not to shrug your shoulders, roll your eyes or start doing something else like playing with the television remote or setting the cushions, etc. while talking about important items with your mates. "I'm not listening to you," kind of gestures can and do worsen the situation.

Nonverbal behaviors constitute as much as 55% of the message sent in interpersonal communications. Good communications make sure the words and the body language match.

Show Respect: As Voltaire put it, "I do not agree with what you have to say, but I'll defend to death your right to say it." Respect the other person's point of view, even if you disagree with it. Respect means listening and accepting their right to have an opinion. It doesn't mean you have to change your own beliefs or points of view. Neither does it mean trying to change your partner's views.

Say "No" to Blame Games: Rather than telling your partner that he or she is the reason you are hurt, it's better to simply express that you are hurting right now. Ask your partner to work with you to make things better so that you tackle problems as a team not trying to change each other as individuals.

Invite your partner to work with you rather than positioning yourselves as adversaries against each other.

"What do we need to do to get out of this problem?" This way both of you can be more open about your emotions and issues that you have and look for solutions together. Also, try using words like "I", "me", "myself" rather than "you", "yours" or "ours."

If fighting does erupt, make sure it's **Fair Fighting**. Here are the rules to follow for that:

- No physical assault

- No name calling.
- Stick to the existing topic. Don't bring up previous issues that you may already have supposedly resolved before.
- Don't dare the other into doing anything.
- No ultimatums or tantrums.
- No sentences that begin with, "If you loved me you would…….."
- Don't threaten to end the marriage in the middle of a fight. If you're finished with the marriage, negotiate that up with your partner when you're calm.
- If you reach a point during a fight where you need a break or some space, specifically ask for the time you need and agree to pick up the topic later at a designated time and place.
- If the topic you need to discuss with your spouse is a hot one, schedule with them a time and location and announce the topic on the agenda before starting. Don't ambush your partner. And make sure to commence and end on time.
- Use the "When you _____ then I _____" format. Be specific about what evoked your feelings or responses.
- If you were hurt by something in particular regarding what your partner had said, then ask exactly what they meant by a specific word or sentence rather than having your own version of what the other might have meant.
- Gratitude goes a long way to sustain health in your body and your relationship. Be grateful and express it to your partner, even in the middle of the fight i.e., "If nothing else dear, I'm grateful that you hang in here with me as we search for solutions. I know I'm not always easy to get along with."

Don't Take the Relationship for Granted

One of the biggest killers of a significant relationship is taking it for granted, which means doing something, repeatedly so many times that it becomes a habit and is then no longer appreciated. For instance, if your partner makes you breakfast everyday then it will eventually become a routine, and you may not thank him or her after a month or two, or don't compliment the food anymore.

Taking your partner for granted leads to neglect of them as a person. Assuming your partner will always be there, assuming your partner knows you want them and appreciate them, assuming that whatever needs to be talked about will eventually come into conversation is like assuming your child will grow and mature in health and you have to do nothing.

Each of us prize being prized. Each of us thrive on the special attention that comes from another person we think is special. All of that wonderful stuff goes out the window when you take any of it for granted.

You can do the following exercise to keep reminding yourself of how much you value your partner:

Valuing Exercise

Take a moment to look at each other and find something you may not have noticed before about that beloved face.

Close your eyes the next time your partner is talking, singing or simply reading your favorite passage or reciting a poem. Concentrate on the tones, color and uniqueness in the voice that you may not have noticed before. Find a word or sentence to give your partner a compliment that you have never given before. Share these new observations with each other. Keep curiosity and the adventure of re-discovering each other alive and regularly activated.

Our brain has the capacity to be highly selective in what we pay attention to, which at times leads us to see only what we want to see. This is called focus. But when selective perception happens below the conscious awareness, you may be missing out on something. There's a reason for the old adage that familiarity breeds contempt or at least boredom. This need not be if you keep exploring who your partner is on multiple levels.

Pledge What You Will Do, Not Only What You Won't Do

After a fight, couples make up and make promises about what they won't do any more. "I won't drink as much", "I won't go shopping as often" or "I won't fight dirty and unfairly with you."

Unfortunately, that's not enough to really make things better. Promises about what you won't do doesn't necessarily get what needs to be done accomplished. For example, if one partner has had an affair and, to start the healing of the relationship, promises to cut off with the other person and stop the affair, that's all well and good. That may begin the process of rebuilding trust.

In addition to that, however, what will the partner do to also improve the relationship? Yes, it's good to stop the infidelity, but the relationship will only begin to heal and grow stronger if the couple also agrees to do several things that pay attention to each other.

If you were to consider a person for employment and they promised they would not show up late, not embezzle your money, and not sexually harass coworkers, would that be enough to qualify them as a viable candidate? Probably not. You also want to know what they would do for you. Would they show up on time? Would they develop the skills to make a profit for you and report others who might be stealing from you? Would they not only refrain from sexual harassment but would they also contribute to positive teambuilding?

Magic Pixie Dust to Improve Your Married Life

There isn't a magic potion to instantaneously make things better between a couple. However, here is one exercise I think is as close to a magic pixie dust as you can get.

This exercise requires resilience and emotional leadership from at least one partner to make it work. Before starting this exercise, make sure that you are able to carry out this exercise without placing any blame on the other person or losing patience.

Here's the Pixie Dust Exercise:

Agree in advance with your partner to do this exercise. Find a quiet place away from distractions and interruptions. It is strongly advised that both of you read this exercise before doing it together.

Step One: With your attention on your spouse repeat to yourself: "Just like me, this person is seeking some happiness for his or her life."

Step Two: With attention on your spouse, repeat to yourself: "Just like me, this person is trying to avoid suffering in his or her life."

Step Three: With attention on your spouse, repeat to yourself: "Just like me, this person has known sadness, loneliness and despair."

Step Four: With attention on your spouse, repeat to yourself: "Just like me this person is seeking to fulfill his or her needs."

Step Five: With attention on your spouse, repeat to yourself: "Just like me, this person is learning about life."

Step Six: With attention on your spouse, repeat to yourself: "Just like me, this person is doing the best they can right now."

One partner should complete all six steps, and then the other person can repeat the same. Make sure that your complete attention is on your spouse and that there aren't any distractions. For extra impact, you can say these things while looking into each other's eyes, holding hands, and perhaps even saying them out loud.

This exercise doesn't need more than 10 to 15 minutes to complete. Once the exercise is finished, leave the room and go to separate places without any further conversation. Write in a diary or journal your feelings and thoughts related to this exercise. Share what you have written with each other. Add talk dialogue as desired.

Repeat this exercise as often as you may need to, especially when you feel that the tension is building up again. Even if it doesn't work the first time, or one or both of you lose your patience or start the blame game again, try repeating it again after a couple of days. You might feel differently.

However, if you feel that the exercise is doing more harm than good and the feelings of blaming, resentment, negativity and anger are only increasing, then it may be time to seek professional help.

Be Kind

You probably know your partner's weaknesses better than anyone else. Couples usually know each other's hot buttons very well. Nothing good comes from pushing those buttons. All you end up doing is causing more fights and troubling issues. Practice hitting the "kind" button with your partner, not the "mean" button. Unless of course you just want to be mean.

Of course, you know the most common reason couples use to be mean to each other? Because the other person was mean to them. And so it goes, spiraling into negativity.

You don't need a good reason to use the kind button other than it's the kind thing to do to someone you profess to love.

The Three "T's"

Make the most of the three T's which have been extensively discussed in this book. The first two are **Touch** and **Talk**. The third T is the **Time** to do the other two: Touch, Talk and Time.

The "Talk" must be about meaningful issues, not just discussions about superficialities such as the news of the day, what the children are doing or neighborhood gossip. Dig deeper with your talk to share your personal expectations, feelings, thoughts, hopes and dreams, not only as a couple, but as individuals.

Talk, significant talk, is what feeds the relationship emotionally. The "Touch" part feeds the relationship physically. Touching may happen in any form or degree from simply holding hands to long, languid lovemaking, so long as both partners consent.

Both of these forms of marriage feeding, however, must be sincere and regular. In America, if it's not scheduled, odds are, it won't happen, whatever it may be. To make sure the Time is carved out for Talk and Touch, schedule it on your calendars!

Counseling/Coaching

Professional counseling can help a relationship solve problems and improve. However, there are deterrents that often delay couples from making that first appointment or even going at all.

I'll grant you, counseling is not for everyone. But there are some attitudes and prejudices about counseling that linger from the old days when counseling was thought to be for weaklings who couldn't solve their own problems. Ironically, many of the same people who say that about emotional and relationship problems, don't hesitate to take their car in for service, call the Cable Guy when the TV doesn't work right or fetch the plumber to unplug the sink. The resistance to getting counseling help for a relationship is not rational.

Prejudices about Counseling: More often than not, asking for marriage counseling means agreeing that there are some problems in the marriage, but many couples don't want to believe that.

There is resistance to letting family, friends or social acquaintances know that things are not just perfect. Even more challenging for a couple can be the thought of opening up and talking about intimate issues with a complete "stranger," the counselor.

There's also the time factor, meaning so many other things come first in the life of busy couples, especially when both work and they are raising young children. The wishful thinking often is why make a big deal out of going to counseling. Probably the relationship problems will take care of themselves over time, anyway, without therapy.

This last attitude is a common, but dangerous way of thinking. A large percentage of the couples I work with have waited too long to repair the damage. Not that something can't be done to make things better, but, for it to work, counseling takes time and commitment to the process. The longer a couple waits, the more major the repair job often is.

What to Look for in a Marriage Counselor: It is better to look for a marriage counselor sooner rather than later when things get out of hand. Here are some things to keep in mind when selecting your marriage counselor.

Ask around or check online about the reputation of the counselor you're considering. Talk with someone who has used marriage counseling and listen to their experience about how they found and worked with the right counselor for them.

Finally, a good and ethical counselor will <u>never</u> do the following things:

- Blame one of you for problems in your relationship.
- Advise you to stay together or break up.
- Embarrass you or your partner or be judgmental.
- Take sides with one of you against the other.
- Ask you to do something which is against your values or beliefs.
- Reveal your personal information to someone else or break confidentiality in any way

What to Expect: At first, therapy can be a bit overwhelming. You have no idea what you are getting into, or what to expect. Here is an outline of my process I use with couples. It can give you an idea of what to expect.

The Beginning
Often, the most difficult step is getting to the marriage counselor's office. It is an unknown territory, both literally and emotionally. Expect to be greeted by a receptionist or the counselor at the door. Usually some paperwork and signing of forms is necessary. As a rule that should take no longer than 15 minutes. If your counselor keeps you waiting longer than that, this may be a red flag and it would be good to ask the counselor if they regularly have difficulty starting on time.

The First Session
The first session is focused on gathering information and getting acquainted with questions about work, children, date of marriage and when and where the couple met. After that, each individual is given the

chance to speak about their thoughts and feelings that might be troubling them about their marriage or relationship. Expect the counselor to take notes.

Hopefully, your counselor will be able at the end of the first session to give you some idea of their thoughts about how counseling can be useful to you. A specific focus for you and your partner to work on is often formulated in the first session.

The Second Session and Going Forward

The next session is used initially to catch up with the couple and to hear about what they've been doing with each other in the interim since the last session. There are often questions that have formulated in my mind after I've gone over the notes from the first session. I will ask the couple to clarify those issues for me.

As needed, the second session digs deeper into family genealogy, patterns in the family that may be affecting the marriage and sources of resentment. Here I begin building a foundation of hope for the couple that their work in marriage counseling will pay off.

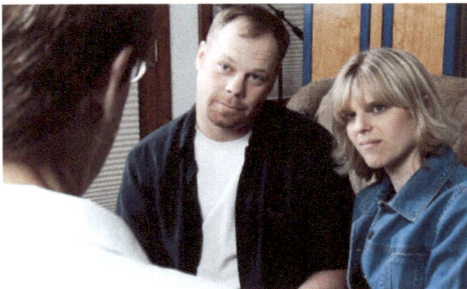

Often in this session, a couple wants to know how long I think it will take them to get what they came for, marital repair and a return to joyful functioning with each other. Of course, there is no set formula or way to answer that question definitively. Nevertheless, it is a valid concern for couples, given that they are taking time and money away from their regular life to focus on their marriage. As a rule, I encourage couples to commit six-months to focus on making significant changes and up to 10 counseling sessions to support them in that work. These parameters, however, will vary from couple to couple.

The second session sets the stage for a variety of activities and assignments from which the couple will benefit. More often than not, homework is given to the couple at the end of the session. Suggestions include books to read, groups to attend, specific skills to practice with each other or personal work that one of the couple needs to do in order to be more available to his or her partner. Other activities can include journaling, regular dialogue, a date night and discussion about blocks in their intimacy.

I repeatedly remind couples that what makes the difference in their marriage will be what they do with each other between counseling sessions, not what happens in counseling. Counseling is like coaching sessions that occur on the sidelines of a sports game. The game stops momentarily so the coach can make some suggestions to the players. Then the game is on again. Improvement in the game will occur only to the extent that players are able to implement in the game what's been talked about in the coaching timeout. And, as with most athletic events, if things are going well, there is no need for extra coaching.

Conclusion
Nothing Changes Unless
Something Changes

Life Is A Beach

One of my favorite bumper stickers from the 70's stated, "Life Is a Beach." At the time, as a graduate student trying to understand human behavior with the overall intention of making the world a better place, I scoffed at this saying. I interpreted it to mean something a lazy person would think, that the point of life is to live with as little effort as possible as close to paradise as one could get.

Now, several decades later, I can interpret the same bumper sticker differently. The beach is a place where opposite forces struggle with each other. In the case of the beach literally, water and land come to some sort of agreement about boundaries and create what is generally thought to be a great place for a vacation.

At another level, the beach metaphorically represents a place where change and status quo war with each other. As human beings, we struggle to resist change and to give birth to it, both at the same time. In fact, both forces are necessary to sustain life.

Old ideas give way to new ideas. At the same time, if ideas change too rapidly, they never mature into useful realities that benefit human life. On the other hand, if nothing ever changes, life becomes stagnant and that is also risky. Too much change is called Chaos, which is destructive. Too little change is called Paralysis or rigor mortis, sometimes known as death.

As far as marriage in America is concerned, maybe the serial monogamy (one marriage after another) pattern that we practice is what we want. Indeed, there are some good things about it. It provides people in one lifetime multiple experiences with multiple partners. It creates a diverse hodgepodge, demonstrating that family life can be accomplished in a variety of ways.

However, the downsides are expensive and painful and often lead to despair that "joyful" and "durable" are two experiences that can't cohabitate in the same relationship.

American marriage is at risk of becoming such a fleeting reality that none of the good things that come out of a long term, healthy and durable relationship can accrue to family members.

Changing Partners But Using The Same Old Dance

If partners change partners but continue using the same patterns of behavior and thought, nothing really changes. Different partners, but we get the same outcomes of experience and results from the same patterns of interaction. Americans love the idea of marriage and pursue it with dedication at great expense. However, we often do not use the skill sets and ideas necessary to make it a successful and meaningful experience.

I've given you here in this book some different and effective ways of looking at your relationship realities. I hope you have the encourage to try them out, experiment with them yourself and see if you and your partner can use them to make for yourselves the quality relationship you want.

Change is not easy

Doing something different from what your family or your neighbors or your church taught you can be risky. It's also risky to find something that works and gives you a better relationship full of joy and fun, unlike those of your family or neighbors or people you go to synagogue with. Even if the new changes are desirable, status quo will resist them.

If you decide to stay in your old comfort zones, I will not judge you. Familiar ways of thinking and functioning can be very tenacious and unyielding.

However, if you want to go for it and try something different to make things better, you may want to use an outside, objective coach or counselor trained to help you get through the difficult and scary phases of change.

Let me know when you're ready to start: Paul W. Anderson, Ph.D.
913-901-9110 or 843-422-1408.

You can also make contact through my website:
www.netpsychologist.com.

References

"Marriage Rules: A Manual For The Married and Coupled Up," Harriet Learner, Ph.D., Gotham Books, 2012.

"Talk to Me Like I'm Someone You Love: Relationship Repair in a Flash," Nancy Dreyfus, Psy.D., Jeremy P. Tarcher, 1993.

"The Secret of Staying in Love: Loving Relationships Through Communication," John Powell, S.J., Thomas More, 1974.

"The Joy Of Sex: A Gourmet Guide to Lovemaking," Alex Comfort, M.B., Ph.D., Penguin Books, 1972. (more recent revisions are available)

www.ingramcontent.com/pod-product-compliance
Lightning Source LLC
Chambersburg PA
CBHW041758040426
42447CB00001B/2